Camping and Hiking

Neil
Champion

Published in 2014 by Wayland

Copyright © Wayland 2014

Wayland   Wayland Australia
338 Euston Road   Level 17/207 Kent Street
London NW1 3BH   Sydney NSW 2000

Senior editor: Debbie Foy
Designer: Rebecca Painter
Photographer: Michael Wicks
Photoshoot co-ordinator: Jon Richards

Acknowledgements:
The author and publisher would like to thank the following people for
participating in our photoshoot: Paul Scholey, Tom Scholey, Bethan
Scholey, Adam Allali, Florence Wilson.

A special thank you to Pete Mann for supplying camping and
hiking equipment.

All photography by Michael Wicks except
5 top Dreamstime.com/Sergey Ilin; 5 bottom Dreamstime.com/Irina
Shoyhet; 8 Dreamstime.com/Soca Waskitha; 18 istockphoto.com/gaffera;
24 Dreamstime.com/Anna Dudko; 28 Dreamstime.com/hmproudlove;
29 Dreamstime.com/Matt Theilen

British Library Cataloguing in Publication Data
Champion, Neil.
Camping and hiking. -- (Get outdoors)
1. Hiking--Juvenile literature.
2. Camping--Juvenile literature.
3. Outdoor life--Juvenile literature.
I. Title II. Series
796.5'1-dc22

ISBN: 978 0 7502 8875 0

First published in 2010 by Wayland

Printed in China

Wayland is a division of Hachette Children's Books,
an Hachette UK company.
www.hachette.co.uk

Note to parents
and teachers:

The website addresses (URLs)
included in this book were
valid at the time of going
to press. However, because
of the nature of the Internet,
it is possible that some
addresses may have
changed, or sites may have
changed or closed down
since publication. While the
Author and Publishers regret
any inconvenience this may
cause the readers, no
responsibility for any such
changes can be accepted
by either the Author or
the Publishers.

Disclaimer:
In preparation of this book,
all due care has been
exercised with regard to the
advice, activities and
techniques depicted. The
Publishers regret that they
can accept no liability for any
loss or injury sustained.
When learning a new sport,
it is important to get expert
tuition and to follow a
manufacturer's advice.

Contents

The world of camping and hiking

Compared with past generations, most of us do very little walking. Instead we use cars, buses and trains to get us around. But by spending time in the countryside you can enjoy fresh air, get your muscles working on a long walk and get to see nature up close. Whether you are planning a short hike or a camping weekend, you are sure to have a few adventures along the way!

What is hiking?

Hiking means adventurous walking, usually in the countryside. You can go on a day hike or one that lasts for several days. The landscape might be gentle, with low hills and easy route-finding, or it might be difficult and remote, such as mountains or desert.

What is camping?

Camping is the art of staying dry, comfortable, fed and watered while living in a tent or other simple shelter. You can camp for a single night or for many weeks on an **expedition**. It is best to start by not going far from home or for very long. As you become more experienced, you might choose to go for longer and further afield.

These hikers are stretching their legs on the hills close to their homes. An experienced adult is walking with them.

Putting the two together

The combination of hiking and camping is a great physical and mental challenge. Because you carry your home and your food on your back, you can get to remote and beautiful places that cannot be reached by any other means. However, you will need to train your body to carry heavy packs, and your muscles and **tendons** to cope with difficult walking **terrain**. You will also need map-reading skills and the ability to use a compass. Cooking over a fire or small stove and pitching a tent in wind and rain are also useful skills to learn!

A peaceful and remote campsite on the shore of a lake surrounded by forest and hills.

A busy campsite in the middle of the woods. You can see a useful washing line strung between two trees!

Walking for fitness

Walking is the most natural exercise. Humans have relied upon their legs to get them around for thousands of years. Practised hikers can cover 48 km (30 miles) a day across rough terrain, but today most of us tend not to walk so much. This means we need to train ourselves for long days out walking in the countryside.

Start locally

The best way to train for hiking is to get out and do small walks around your local area, to build up your stamina. As you become fitter, aim to walk for longer and carry a heavier pack. You also get to test your kit – walking shoes or boots, your rucksack and your waterproofs. You might also start to learn how to **navigate**. If you get it wrong, at least you are in your own neighbourhood.

These young hikers are showing good team work by helping each other across a stream.

Before you go

There are exercises you can do before you start walking. For example, while you are at home you could step up and down a stair or step 50 times. Now try adding a rucksack and do the same again. Or when you are out in the countryside you can do stretching exercises just before you start on your walk. The muscles you use performing these exercises are the same ones you will use going up a hill or mountainside.

Gentle stretching is important for before and after exercise. Here, the large thigh muscles are being worked on.

This stretch will help the calf muscles as well as the thighs recover from hard use.

The Walking Man

An American called Gary Hause is one of the world's great walkers. He set out to walk the globe. It took him 87 days to walk across America and 147 days to do the same in Europe.

A British long-distance walker hiked from South America to Prudhoe Bay in Alaska. He covered the amazing distance of 30,000 km (19,000 miles) in just 2,425 days!

Hiking and camping are easy activities to get involved in. If you are lucky, your family or friends might already be participating. There may also be clubs at school and in your local community that can help you find your feet.

Taking the first step

Finding a group of experienced people who can guide you on your first hiking and camping trips is very important. These could be parents or club leaders, such as the scouts or guides. Your school may have an outdoor pursuits club, run by an experienced teacher. Whichever route you take, learn well from those who you trust. They will pass on knowledge about safety, navigation and making good decisions, for example about when to turn back in the face of bad weather.

Scouts and Guides

The Scouts started in Britain in 1907. Lord Baden-Powell ran a camp for 20 boys on Brownsea Island on the south coast. Today there are scout troops all over the world with about 28 million young people actively involved.

The Girl Guides started in 1909 and is now an international organisation with around 326,000 members in the UK.

Hiking and camping are central activities for scouts and guides, with badges to be won for campcraft and cooking skills.

Going on an organised camping trip with a group is a great way to learn campcraft and meet new people.

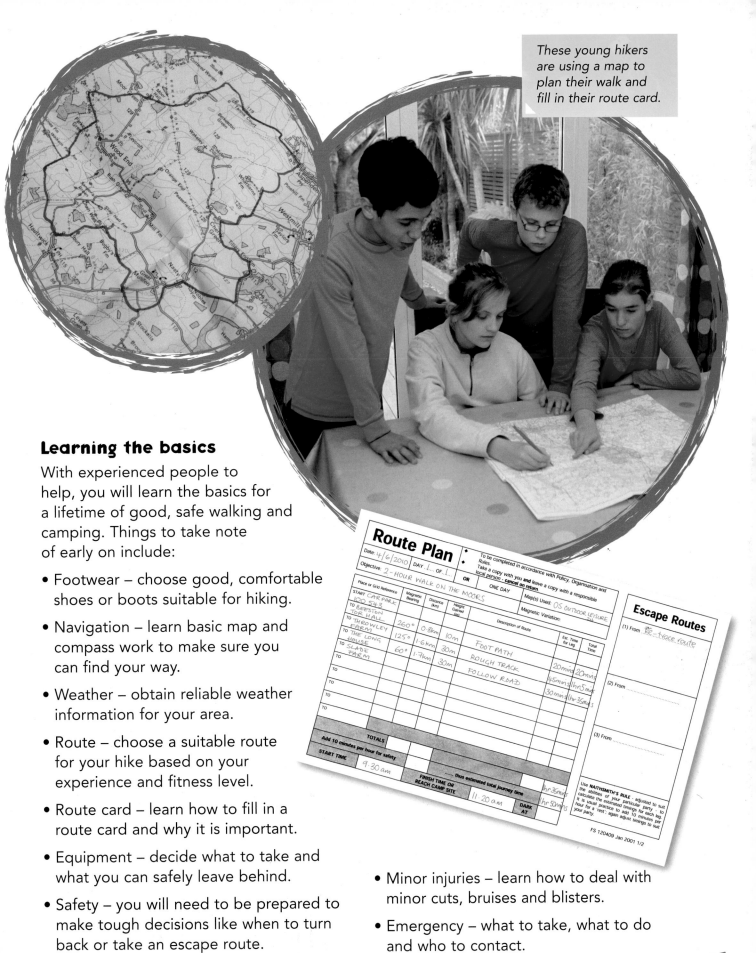

Learning the basics

With experienced people to help, you will learn the basics for a lifetime of good, safe walking and camping. Things to take note of early on include:

- Footwear – choose good, comfortable shoes or boots suitable for hiking.

- Navigation – learn basic map and compass work to make sure you can find your way.

- Weather – obtain reliable weather information for your area.

- Route – choose a suitable route for your hike based on your experience and fitness level.

- Route card – learn how to fill in a route card and why it is important.

- Equipment – decide what to take and what you can safely leave behind.

- Safety – you will need to be prepared to make tough decisions like when to turn back or take an escape route.

- Minor injuries – learn how to deal with minor cuts, bruises and blisters.

- Emergency – what to take, what to do and who to contact.

Route Plan

Date: 4/6/2010 DAY ..1.. OF ..1..

Objective: 2-HOUR WALK ON THE MOORS

To be completed in accordance with Policy, Organisation and Rules.
Take a copy with you **and** leave a copy with a responsible local person - **cancel on return.**

OR ONE DAY

Map(s) Used: O.S OUTDOOR LEISURE 24

Magnetic Variation:

Place or Grid Reference	Magnetic Bearing	Distance (km)	Height Gained (m)	Description of Route	Est. Time for Leg	Total Time
START CAR PARK 100 543						
TO BEESTON TOR HALL	260°	0.8km	10m			
TO THROWLEY FARM	125°	1.6km	30m	FOOT PATH		
TO THE LONG HOUSE	60°	1.7km	30m	ROUGH TRACK	20mins	20mins
TO SLADE FARM				FOLLOW ROAD	45mins	1hr 5mins
TO					30mins	1hr 35mins
TO						
TO						
TO						
TOTALS						

Add 10 minutes per hour for safety

START TIME 9:30 am

FINISH TIME **OR** REACH CAMP SITE 11:20 am

.... thus estimated total journey time 1hr 36mins 1hr 50mins

DARK AT

Escape Routes

(1) From Re-trace route

(2) From

(3) From

Use **NAITHSMITH'S RULE** - adjusted to suit the abilities of your particular party - to calculate the estimated timings for each leg. It is usual practice to add 10 minutes per hour for a 'rest'; again adjust timings to suit your party.

FS 120409 Jan 2001 1/2

Equipment for hiking

The right clothing and equipment for keeping you comfortable and safe in all kinds of weather conditions (from warm and sunny, to wet and windy) is vital for a successful day out hiking.

The layering system

One of the key elements to staying comfortable in any weather is by using the layering system. This works in summer and winter, in desert or mountains. The idea is to take lots of thin layers rather than one or two thick items of clothing. This means you can put on or take off warm layers depending upon how hot or cold you might be.

Base layers – these are thin cotton (for summer) or thin wool or artificial fabrics (for cooler temperatures) that go next to your skin. They should be comfortable, light and 'breathable' to allow sweat to pass through.

Mid layers – these can include a sweatshirt, thin jumper or fleece shirt. You might spend all day in a base layer with a mid layer on top, only taking the mid layer off when it gets very warm.

Boots – choose a well-fitting, comfortable pair made from leather. Walking shoes are fine to wear, but if you are going into rough country, you will need the ankle support you get from boots.

Ready for action, wearing good, strong boots with ankle support, quick-drying windproof trousers and a light and warm fleece.

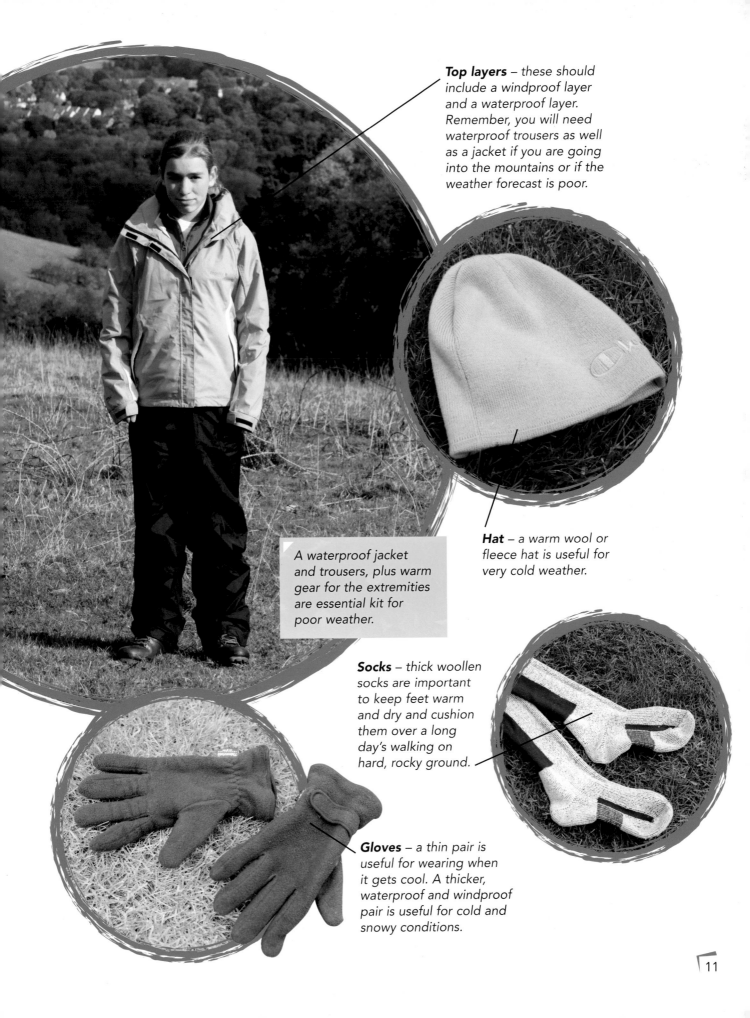

Top layers – these should include a windproof layer and a waterproof layer. Remember, you will need waterproof trousers as well as a jacket if you are going into the mountains or if the weather forecast is poor.

A waterproof jacket and trousers, plus warm gear for the extremities are essential kit for poor weather.

Hat – a warm wool or fleece hat is useful for very cold weather.

Socks – thick woollen socks are important to keep feet warm and dry and cushion them over a long day's walking on hard, rocky ground.

Gloves – a thin pair is useful for wearing when it gets cool. A thicker, waterproof and windproof pair is useful for cold and snowy conditions.

Equipment for camping

Camping should be a fun, enjoyable experience. To make sure that it is, you will need to choose your camping kit wisely. Get advice from experienced campers before buying your tent or sleeping bag. There are many designs to choose from and they should match your needs.

Choosing a tent

First think carefully about how you will be using your tent. Will you be camping with your family on a lowland campsite, using a car to transport everything? Or will you be camping out in the wilds, with a group of friends or members of a club, carrying everything on your back? Tents range from lightweight, single-person backpacking models to much heavier, six-person family styles. Some are designed to withstand storms in the mountains while others are for gentle, valley camping.

A two-person domed tent. A good choice for general camping trips.

Domed tent – *a popular design for family tents. It is easy to put up but generally heavy.*

'A' Frame or Ridge tent – *an old design, strong and stable, but not much space inside.*

A ridge tent is still popular with outdoor organisations as it is sturdy and hardwearing.

Tunnel tent – *this design gives the best inside space and is quick to put up.*

Geodesic tent – *strong and stable with a good inside space. The best design for mountains and bad weathe*

Choosing a sleeping bag

Your choice of sleeping bag depends on how cold it might get in the places you plan to camp. Sleeping bags are rated by 'seasons'. One season is the lightest and least warm; five seasons is the heaviest and the warmest. They can be made from artificial fibres (cheap, heavy but warm, even when wet) or down (expensive, light, long-lasting, but no good when wet). Mummy-shaped sleeping bags are warmer and lighter than other shapes. You will also need a sleeping mat to go underneath your sleeping bag.

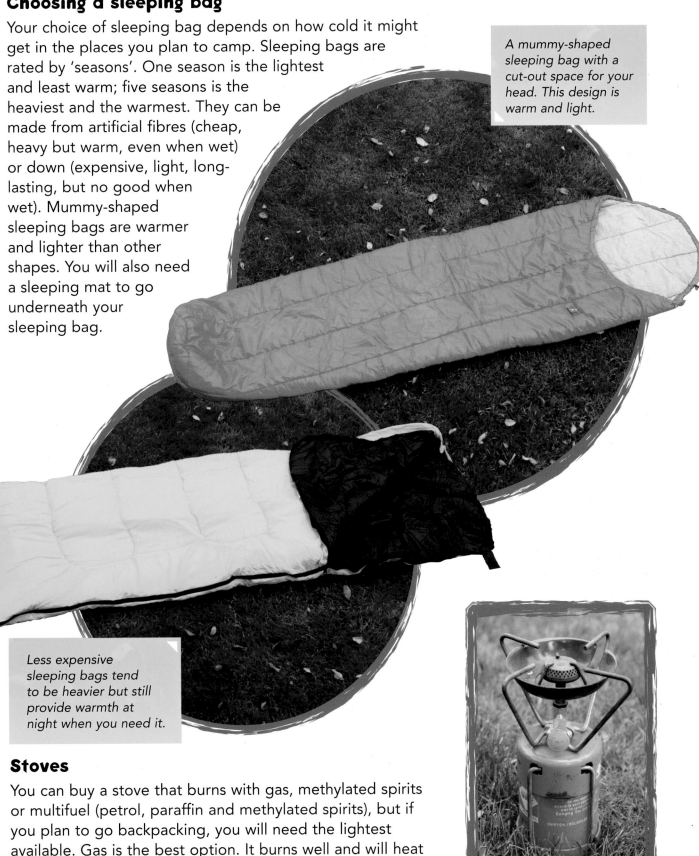

A mummy-shaped sleeping bag with a cut-out space for your head. This design is warm and light.

Less expensive sleeping bags tend to be heavier but still provide warmth at night when you need it.

Stoves

You can buy a stove that burns with gas, methylated spirits or multifuel (petrol, paraffin and methylated spirits), but if you plan to go backpacking, you will need the lightest available. Gas is the best option. It burns well and will heat water and cook food quickly.

Packing your rucksack

It may seem like a simple task, but you need to learn the best way to pack a rucksack. Here are some handy hints on packing all you need for a day's walking in your local area, or a longer camping hike in the wilderness.

The size of your rucksack

Rucksacks are measured by **volume** in litres (L). A good size for a day rucksack is between 30 and 40 L. A multi-day rucksack will be larger – 55 L up to about 80 L. However, you must consider just how much weight you can carry, too. As a rule, never carry more than one third of your body weight and up to 15 kg (33 lb) as a maximum.

The gear needed for a short camping trip includes sleeping bag and mat, spare clothes, cooking equipment and food, map, compass, first aid kit and emergency whistle.

Packing your rucksack

Getting this right can make a big difference to how comfortable your back will feel after a couple of hours of walking. Here are some top tips:

- Make sure the rucksack sits on your hips and is close to your body and shoulders. A good make of rucksack will come in several different back sizes. Get one that fits you and allows you to maintain a good **posture**.

- Make sure you pack it correctly. Heavy items near the top will give you greater stability when walking.

- Pack things that you might need in the outside pockets or near the top of the sack – lunch, water, map and compass, first aid kit, waterproof clothes.

- If you are carrying a stove with liquid fuel, make sure it is kept away from food and wrap it well in plastic bags.

- Always do up the rucksack's waist buckle and tighten it.

- Try not to have things hanging off the outside of your rucksack as they will affect your balance.

- Make your sack as light as possible! Never take more than you need for safety and comfort on your trip.

A well-packed rucksack should sit comfortably on the hips and shoulders.

Waterproofing your rucksack

No rucksack is completely waterproof. So, to prevent your sleeping bag or spare clothing getting wet, wrap them securely inside a strong plastic bag or waterproof rucksack liners.

How to walk

Walking in wild places is not really about speed. It is more to do with saving energy to use over a long day's hiking. It is also about adapting to the ground under your feet – steep grassy slopes, rocky paths and sandy dunes. Injury to the legs (especially twisting ankles and knees) is the most common among walkers. Good technique and supportive footwear will help you avoid this.

When walking over easy ground, you should aim to get a good rhythm in your stride. Strike with your heel to get a good grip and avoid a slip.

Adapting to different terrain takes skill. Make sure your boot wedges between wet and slippery rocks to avoid a slip.

Get the rhythm

A good rhythm is key to good walking. This means having your **centre of gravity** over your feet, keeping your hands free for balance and using the natural swing of your hips and legs to move rather than over-using your muscles. You will have to constantly adapt to changes underfoot. Doing this while keeping your rhythm is important, as stumbling and losing your balance take lots of energy to correct.

It is important to keep a good steady pace and remember not to leave the slowest of the group behind.

Trekking poles in use, adding stability and saving energy for this young hiker.

Pace

Keeping up a constant pace is important. Speeding up and then slowing down takes more energy than moving along at an even speed. Walking requires a slow burn of energy. Pacing yourself so that you have energy to spare at the end of the day is the trick. Avoid stopping and starting. If you need to drink some water or tie your laces, try to do them at the same stop. This way you won't have to stop again for an hour or so.

Foot position

The sole of your boot or shoe is your contact with the ground. It should be firm and confident. The foot alters its grip to suit the terrain, as will your body position. For example, while coming steeply down hill, you should dig your heels into the slope and have your centre of balance over your feet by slightly bending your knees.

Trekking poles

Trekking poles can be very useful for hilly areas and give you lots of stability. They can also take strain from your leg muscles and knees.

Planning your trip

You have joined a club, bought some outdoor kit, and been out on some long day walks. Now you are ready to plan your first camping expedition. Where should you go, what should you take and what planning should you do?

Your first campsite

An official campsite is likely to make your first experience of camping a good one. There will be taps with fresh water for cooking and drinking, and probably a toilet and shower block. Hygiene is very important, so make sure you always wash your hands before handling food.

This is a well-organised official campsite that offers campers toilet and wash facilities as well as a car park.

Route cards

Filling in a route card will help you focus on the walk ahead of you. Think about how far you might want to go. Roughly 9–12 km (6–8 miles) would be a reasonable first day. Study your map. How much uphill will there be? (count the **contours**). Will you have to cross streams or find a way round rocky areas? Find out how long it should take to walk back to the campsite. You can do this using Naithsmith's Rule.

These two young hikers are filling in their route card, having planned their walk and worked out all the distances and grid references involved.

Modern technology can help all hikers. A global positioning system (GPS) is used for navigation and the Internet (right) is the best way to obtain a weather forecast.

Naithsmith's Rule

Naithsmith was a Victorian mountaineer. He worked out a rule for estimating how long a day's hike might take based on the distance you travel, the speed you walk at, and the hills you have to climb. He said that on average you walk at 5 km (3 miles) an hour plus half an hour for every 300 m (1,000 ft) of **ascent**. This can depend on your overall fitness, the weight of your rucksack, the weather conditions and what the ground is like underfoot.

Weather forecasts

Checking the weather forecast before you go is vital! Today the Internet is the best option. You will usually find a written description of the weather, a description using symbols (for cloud, rain, snow, sun) and **synoptic** weather charts. Try to get a forecast for five days ahead.

Choosing a campsite

Whether you are hiking to an official campsite or planning on camping in the wild, you should have an idea of what to look for to make a good pitch for your tent.

Choosing a campsite

The main things to consider when locating your campsite are:

• Stick to level ground – you don't want to be sleeping on a slope!

• Stay fairly close to a source of fresh water such as a tap or stream.

• Look out for raised ground as it drains well after rain. A small **hillock** is ideal, for example.

• Don't camp under trees as dead branches can fall off in high winds, and leaves will drip water onto your tent long after rain has passed.

• Work out the **prevailing** wind direction and pitch your tent facing away from it.

This pair have chosen a good site for their tent. It is on level, well-drained ground, away from trees but sheltered from the prevailing wind.

A tidy tent with cooking gear just outside ready for use, and a source of water not far away.

Camp organisation

Once your tent is pitched, place your sleeping mat and sleeping bag ready for the night. You can use spare clothing as a pillow. Make sure your torch is handy – before it gets dark and you can't find it! Organise a cooking area close to your tent but not inside it, and ideally down wind of it. Collect fresh water from a clean source – such as a tap, if available. If you are wild camping, it will be from a stream. You are now ready to boil the water to make hot drinks and for cooking your evening meal.

Make sure you boil and sterilise water not taken from a tap.

Pollution

If you are camping in the wild, make sure your water is from a clean source. All water should be flowing (from a river or stream), never **stagnant** (a pond, for example). Wash your hands and clean your teeth downstream from where you collect your drinking water. Try to use **biodegradable** soap and washing-up liquid. Make sure your **latrine** is sited well away from the water.

Food, water and cooking

You have pitched your tent securely and organised your kit. Now it's time to get cooking! Safety and hygiene are very important in camp cooking. It is easy to let your utensils become dirty, so make sure you take extra care in keeping them clean.

Water

If you are taking your water from a stream, you should purify or filter it to remove harmful bugs. The easiest way to purify water is to boil it for about 10 minutes. You can buy chlorine purification tablets at good outdoor shops, but they can make the water taste funny. Filters will remove grit from your water. A combination of filtering and boiling should make water safe to drink.

Utensils *like these can be neatly stored on a ring so that they don't go missing.*

Chlorine sterilising tablets should be added to water to kill off any harmful bugs.

Use water bottles to store purified water.

Cooking a meal is one of the highlights of the day. Ensure your lit stove is kept away from the tent.

Water for life

About 60% of our body weight is water. Becoming **dehydrated** can really affect your physical performance. It is best to sip mouthfuls of water rather than become thirsty and drink lots in one go. When you are walking all day with a heavy pack, you will need to increase your intake from about 2 L (3½ pt) a day to 3 L (5 pt) or even more.

Food and cooking

Most of us need between 2,000 and 2,500 **kilocalories** a day to keep healthy and active. When you are hiking you are using extra energy, so you will need to increase this to around 3,500 kilocalories. Today there are many good meals that you can buy ready cooked and just re-heat. Good alternatives are pasta or rice dishes. Make sure you are eating plenty of **carbohydrates**, as well as some fat and protein.

Warning – cooking can be hazardous. Never cook inside your tent as it can catch fire easily, and always make sure that an adult helps you!

23

Hazards on the hill

There are many things to watch out for when you are out in the countryside hiking or camping. These include getting lost, coming across swollen rivers, boggy ground or steep cliffs, falling rocks, getting stung or bitten, and injury to yourself or others.

Looking at risk

Make a list of the **hazards** you might come across. How likely are they to happen? Who would be at risk? What would you need to do? For example, injuring an ankle on rough ground could happen. The person then may need help to move. Do you have a mobile phone or radio and do you know who to call?

International distress signals

The international emergency telephone number is 112. However, you may not get a mobile phone signal in the countryside. In this instance, use your emergency whistle and make six blasts on it (in the dark, use your torch and make six flashes). Now wait for one minute and then make six more blasts. Keep doing this until you hear the return signal of three blasts from a rescue party.

This hiker has come across a common hazard in the mountains – a cliff edge.

Getting lost

Always travel with experienced people who know how to navigate well. Learn how to read a map and use a compass to find north and take a **bearing**. If you do become lost, don't panic. Think back to the last place you knew where you were. Find this on your map. Now try to **relocate** yourself by piecing together what you have done since then (walked into the sun, crossed a river, went through a forest, and so on) and try to find your route on the map, too. This way you should be able to relocate yourself.

Knowing how to use a map and compass are essential skills for the hiker and camper. Make sure you learn!

Deep or fast flowing rivers are a major hazard. Never try to cross them. Always look for a bridge or another way around.

Other hazards

Never cross swollen or deep rivers as they can carry you away. It is far better to look for a bridge or even wait until the river has gone down. Avoid bogs and marshes and if you do have to cross them, do not go alone. Move between safe 'islands' of vegetation. Never climb or descend cliffs. Better safe than sorry!

Hikers' first aid

Hikers need to know how to deal with simple injury or illness when out in the countryside. Here are some of the most common problems that you may have to tackle.

Cuts and sprains

Small cuts should be cleaned with water and antiseptic and covered with a plaster or dressing. Check and change the plasters or dressings regularly.

Sprains are common to the ankle and knee. The injured person should be sat down. You can help a minor sprain by putting the injured part on ice or into cold running water. Keep cold for around five minutes. Then repeat again. The cold will help reduce the swelling. After a while, wrap the injured area in a bandage to compress the injury – but not so tight it stops the blood flow. Finally get the injured person to raise the limb. It all comes down to ICE – ice, compression, **elevation**.

A first aid kit should contain all the things you are most likely to need – including plasters, tweezers, antiseptic, wound dressings and scissors.

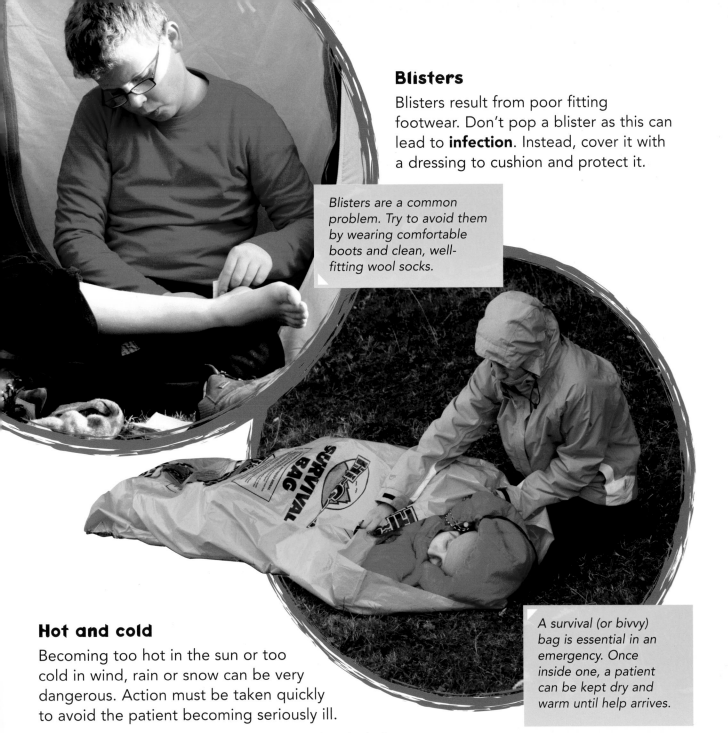

Blisters

Blisters result from poor fitting footwear. Don't pop a blister as this can lead to **infection**. Instead, cover it with a dressing to cushion and protect it.

Blisters are a common problem. Try to avoid them by wearing comfortable boots and clean, well-fitting wool socks.

A survival (or bivvy) bag is essential in an emergency. Once inside one, a patient can be kept dry and warm until help arrives.

Hot and cold

Becoming too hot in the sun or too cold in wind, rain or snow can be very dangerous. Action must be taken quickly to avoid the patient becoming seriously ill.

Signs of someone becoming overheated include being thirsty, tired, unstable on their feet and hot, with a fast heartbeat. In this case, stop, get them into the shade, give them water and perhaps a salty snack. Dab their neck and face with cold water to cool them.

Signs of someone becoming too cold include shivering, tiredness, strange behaviour, quietness or even slurred speech. In this case, stop, get them into shelter – put up your tent or get out an emergency **bivvy bag**. Put them into a sleeping bag and plenty of clothing. After a while encourage them to eat some food and have a hot drink.

First aid

Remember, the first principle of all first aid is not to make a patient's condition worse. If you do not know what is wrong or how to help, it is best to do nothing other than get help as quickly as possible.

Great hikes around the world

There are many fantastic hiking trails around the world. See what you can find in your area. Good places to start looking are your local library or on the Internet.

Sometimes trails will be very long, but you can walk just one small part – for a day's outing or a weekend camping trip. You should always get advice on any trail you want to try out, as some are very remote. Try to go with people who have walked the trail or path before. Enjoy the challenge!

Hiking in Britain

Britain has a great mix of mountains, hills, moors and beautiful coastlines. Refer to an Ordnance Survey map for well-known trails and footpaths.

Popular with hikers are:

- The Pembrokeshire coastal footpath. This has some of the most stunning coastal scenery in Britain.

- The Pennine Way. This is one of the most travelled footpaths in the UK.

Fine views over the hills of the Snowdonia National Park in North Wales.

The magnificent mountains of Yosemite National Park in California, provide some of the greatest hiking trails in the United States.

Hiking in North America

North America has many long and scenic trails for you to enjoy. You can often find all the information out about them from park ranger services.

• The Appalachian Trail. This stunning and popular hiking trail has hundreds of campsites, shelters and huts along the way.

• The Great Divide Trail. Another stunning trail, this one is located in Canada and is popular with hikers and campers alike.

Hiking in Australia

Australia is a flat, dry **continent** with some of the world's most poisonous animals. You need to know where is safe to go and what to take with you.

• Australian Alps Walking Track. This trail takes you through some beautiful scenery in south-eastern Australia.

• The Tasmanian Trail. Tasmania is a large island off the south-east coast of Australia and has stunning scenery.

Glossary

Ascent   In hiking terms this means climbing uphill.

Bearing   A reading in degrees, taken from a compass and used as line of direction in which to walk. Bearings are between 1 and 360 degrees, making up a complete circle.

Biodegradable   Materials that can be broken down into smaller particles and re-used in the natural cycle.

Bivvy bag   A lightweight waterproof survival bag. It is large enough for one person and their rucksack to get some shelter from bad weather.

Carbohydrates   Energy foods, such as bread, pasta, rice, potatoes and cakes. Wholegrain bread, rice and pasta release their energy slowly and so are better for you than quick release foods such as sugary sweets.

Centre of gravity   This is a point where our weight is equally distributed. It is found just below the naval (belly button) in most people.

Continent   One of the seven great blocks of land that make up our planet – North America, South America, Africa, Asia, Australasia, Europe and Antarctica.

Contours   Lines drawn on a map that show areas of equal height above sea level. Most walking maps have a difference of 10 m (30 ft) between each contour line.

Dehydrated   Having too little water inside your body for it to work properly. Mild dehydration will make you thirsty. Your reactions won't be as fast as normal and your muscles won't work as well. Severe dehydration can be extremely serious.

Elevation   Bringing something into a higher position.

Expedition   A planned and organised journey, usually with some big aim in mind. For example, to climb a mountain, explore a jungle or cross a desert to reach a remote spot.

Hazards   Something that could cause harm or injury to you or your group is a hazard. This might include steep cliffs, a river, rock fall, poisonous animals, lightning and so on.

Hillock   A small hill or mound.

Infection   Something that can cause illness through bacteria or a virus. For example, a cut can become infected if it is not treated properly.

Kilocalories   A measure of the energy in food. One kilocalorie is equal to 1,000 calories.

Latrine   A temporary toilet made when out camping. It is usually a screen of canvas with a deep hole dug into the ground.

Navigate   The skill of using a map and compass to find your way over unknown landscapes.

Posture   The shape that our bodies make. There is good posture (that supports our back, hips and knees) and poor posture (slouching, for example).

Prevailing (wind)   The most usual direction for the wind to blow from is said to be the prevailing wind. This will vary depending on where in the world you are.

Relocate   The navigational skill of being able to find your position even though you are lost. To do this you need to use your eyes, memory, map and compass.

Stagnant   Water that does not move or get replaced very often is said to be stagnant. Small ponds and bogs are stagnant. You should not drink from stagnant water as it often contains harmful bugs.

Synoptic (chart)   A weather map that shows areas of low pressure and high pressure, wind direction and speed.

Tendons   Special fibres found in our bodies that attach our muscles to our bones.

Terrain   The particular landscape we are walking in. It might be rocky terrain, desert, marshy or grassy fields, for example.

Utensils   Things we use around the kitchen are often called utensils. This would include pots and pans, spoons, knives and wooden spatulas.

Volume   The space something takes up or has inside it. For example, the volume of a rucksack is measured in litres – this give an idea of how big the rucksack is and how much gear it can carry.

Further information

Books to read

Adventure Outdoors: Wild Trail: Hiking and Camping, Neil Champion
Franklin Watts (2014)

Collins Complete Hiking and Camping Manual: The Essential Guide to Comfortable Walking, Cooking and Sleeping, Rick Curtis, Collins (2007)

The Complete Practical Guide to Camping, Hiking and Wilderness Skills, Peter G Drake, Lorenz (2005)

Useful contacts

The British Mountaineering Council (BMC)
www.thebmc.co.uk

The Scouts Association
www.scouts.org.uk

The Ramblers' Association
www.ramblers.org.uk

Backpackers Club (UK)
www.backpackersclub.co.uk

Camping and Caravanning Club UK
www.campingandcaravanningclub.co.uk

Websites

http://www.hikingaustralia.com.au

This website features all types of hikes from all over Australia.

http://www.campsites-uk.co.uk

This website features a directory of campsites and camping in the UK.

http://www.campcanada.com

This website features a directory of campsites and camping in Canada.

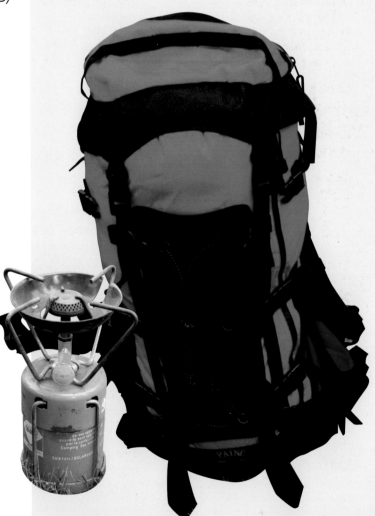

index